Orville & Wilbur Wright

...Step Out Into the Sky.

BY CAROLE MARSH

Copyright © 2002 Carole Marsh

Published by

GALLOPADE™
INTERNATIONAL

800-536-2GET
www.gallopade.com

CAROLE MARSH BOOKS

Gallopade is proud to be a member of these educational organizations and associations:

The National School Supply and Equipment Association
The National Council for the Social Studies

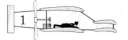

Other Carole Marsh Books

My First Pocket Guide to North Carolina
My First Pocket Guide to Ohio
The Big North Carolina Reproducible Activity Book
The Big Ohio Reproducible Activity Book
The Nifty North Carolina Coloring Book!
The Out-of-This-world Ohio Coloring Book!
My First Book About North Carolina!
My First Book About Ohio!
North Carolina Jeopardy: Answers & Questions About Our State
Ohio Jeopardy: Answers & Questions About Our State
North Carolina "Jography!": A Fun Run Through Our State
Ohio "Jography!": A Fun Run Through Our State

The Mystery of the Biltmore House
The Mystery of the Biltmore Teacher's Resource Book

The Cape Hatteras Lighthouse
The Cape Hatteras Lighthouse Activity Kit

The Lost Colony Storybook
Mystery of the Lost Colony

Blackbeard's Missing Head Mystery

Carolina Christmas
Carolina Christmas Trivia

Table of Contents

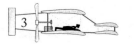

A Word From the Author

I always wanted to be a member of the Man Will Never Fly Society. (Yes, there is such a thing!) Why did I want to join? Because it seemed so silly to think that "man would never fly." After all, people were constantly figuring out how to do all kinds of so-called impossible things—why not flying?!

That's just how two young brothers—Orville and Wilbur—felt. They weren't the first to try to fly, but they became the first to fly a craft "for real," as we might say today. And the rest, as we also say, is history!: airplanes, helicopters, rockets to the moon, space shuttles, and more.

The Wright Brothers and their amazing achievement teach us many important things:

- How to have a dream and stick to it!
- How to succeed no matter what your educational level!
- How hard work pays off!

What society would you like to join today? "No Peace in Our Time." "People Will Never Cure Cancer." "Intolerance Forever." WOULDN'T YOU LIKE TO PROVE THEM ALL WRONG?!

The Wright Brothers did just that, and aren't we glad! After all, it's a really, really long drive from Denver (for example) to Disneyworld. But it's a really short flight—thanks to the Wright Brothers!

A Timeline of Events

 4th century B.C.E.
The kite is invented in China.

 c. 875 C.E.
A Spanish doctor attaches wings to his body and flies, but crashes because he failed to make tailfeathers!

 1485–1500
Italian artist, Leonardo da Vinci, designs a number of muscle-powered "ornithopters."

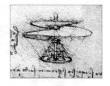

 1678
A Frenchman attempts to fly using "flappers." It was a flop!

 November 21, 1783
First successful flight in a hot air balloon.

 Early 1800s
In England, George Cayley designs early airplanes and helicopters.

 Mid-to-late 1800s
Many people design, test, fly, fail to fly, and crash many different types of "air craft"!

December 17, 1903
Orville and Wilbur Wright become the first to achieve flight in a heavier-than-air plane, using power, that lasts more than a few seconds, is controlled across distance, and successfully landed!

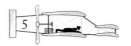

Orville and Wilbur Wright
Step Out Into the Sky!

It is a cold winter's day. It is, in fact, December 17, 1903—a day that will go down in history. But brothers Orville and Wilbur Wright do not care about that at the moment.

Standing on the gigantic sand dune called Kill Devil Hill in Kitty Hawk, North Carolina, the two brothers shiver in the icy wind. They traipse across the blowing sand to the *Flyer*, their flying machine. At least they are counting on it to fly . . . this time.

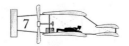

It is Orville's turn to fly the plane. He cranks up the engine of the rather rickety-looking contraption that to some, perhaps, appears more an overgrown toy crafted of fabric and sticks. Like two gentlemen bidding one another farewell on a journey, the brothers shake hands.

Orville stretches out face-down on the bottom wing. Wilbur holds the tip of the wing steady. One of their helpers from the nearby Life Saving Station releases the wire that holds *Flyer* to the frozen ground.

Instantly, *Flyer* begins to roll forward on its launching rail. Faster, faster, ever faster, until—EUREKA!—the craft is aloft . . . moving through the sky . . . heading into history. At last, at last success!

The flight lasted only 12 seconds. The plane flew just 120 feet (37 meters). Nonetheless, it was the first time that any machine carrying a person had raised itself by its own power into the air in full flight. The story of how this world- and history-changing achievement came to be is an amazing tale of two determined brothers.

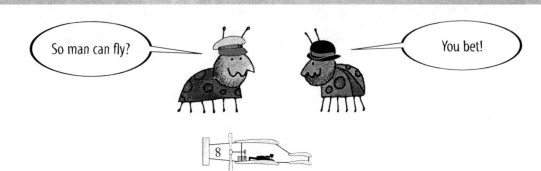

So man can fly?

You bet!

8

Two Brothers, One Dream: "Let's Fly!"

How did Orville and Wilbur Wright get the idea for creating some kind of airplane that would really fly? The seed of this idea was planted in their mind when they were very young!

Orville at 4 years old (left) and Wilbur at 9 years old.

The two young brothers grew up far away from the windblown North Carolina coast in Dayton, Ohio. One day, when Orville was seven-years-old and Wilbur was eleven, their father came home from a business trip. Like many Dads, he had taken the time to buy them a "treat." This surprise was a toy helicopter!

Make a photocopy of this pattern. Put the "aircraft" together as shown. Do you feel sort of Orvilly and Wilbury?

Your finished helicopter will look like this!

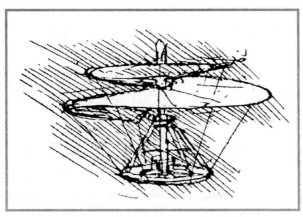

A helicopter sketch by the famous artist Leonardo daVinci.

Cut line

Fold line

Cut line

Add a paper clip to the bottom of your helicopter.

Fold line

Fold line

Fold line

The Wright Stuff?

You may assume that the Wright brothers were two little geniuses who loved school and made all A's—not so! The boys were very bright. They did go to school, of course, but they hated being confined to desks all day long. It is likely that they were "gifted and talented" but not the kind of kids who learn as well in the classroom as they could experimenting with things on their own, which is exactly what they did.

See If You Have the Wright Stuff!

Conduct the following experiments and record your results.

EXPERIMENT	RESULTS
1 Take a ruler and hold it up as high as you can. Let it go.	This is an example of: a. ___ pitch b. ___ yaw c. ___ gravity
2 Take a handkerchief and hold the 4 corners together. Twirl around and see if you can fill the handkerchief with air.	The shape the handkerchief made when filled with air was: a. ___square b. ___curved c. ___flat
3 Get a piece of bendable material such as a chopstick or a drinking straw. Bend it as much as you can without risking it breaking.	Why would something that can bend with the force of the air be important to creating an early airplane? a. ___It is more like a wing and can get lift b. ___It shouldn't bend; it should be stiff

Hmmm! This is very interesting!

Bicycles Built by Two!

So, how did the two young adult brothers make a living for themselves? Wilbur hoped to be an inventor. Orville opened a print shop. Guess what? Neither had much success! In fact, they were going broke when they had a brainstorm: "Let's open a bicycle shop!"

In those days, bicycles were a common mode of transportation as well as the best Christmas present under the tree for kids. Since the brothers were such excellent mechanics, they made a real success of their popular bike shop. In fact, they designed a very sturdy bike that could be made for less money than any other bicycle on the market at that time—a surefire recipe for success!

As you might imagine, while tinkering with tools and spokes and wheels and motion and speed, the brothers added to their knowledge of how to make things "go."

Match the machine on the left with what makes it "go" on the right!

1. bicycle   a. ___ rocket booster

2. glider   b. ___ jet engine, jet fuel

3. hot air balloon   c. ___ tanks of gas

4. early airplane   d. ___ wind

5. space shuttle   e. ___ chain and gears

6. jet airplane   f. ___ engine, gasoline

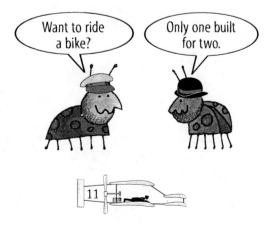

Birds, Bees, Kites, Trees!

During the winter months, Orville and Wilbur had a lot of spare time on their hands. They devoted this time to studying one subject: flight. Like most entrepreneurs, they started right out their own back door. They studied the birds that flew over their yard. The brothers came to this conclusion: "We could not understand that there was anything about a bird that would enable it to fly that could not be built on a larger scale and used by man." To test their theory, they began to build kites. But this was not play to the brothers Wright! Building kites was just one of their many stepping stones to understanding the problems of flight, and evaluating the possibility that they could some day built an aircraft that could fly under its own power with a person aboard!

Build Your Own Diamond Kite!

HERE'S WHAT YOU WILL NEED:

❶ 2 lightweight sticks (24" long)

❷ bread or trash bag ties or some other lightweight wire

❸ a full sheet of newspaper

❹ cellophane or masking tape

❺ a pair of scissors

❻ lightweight string (kite string)

❼ a strip of fabric or party streamers or a ribbon (This is for the tail and should be about 48" to keep your kite from spinning out of control.)

12"

6"

25"

24"

21"

FULL SHEET OF NEWSPAPER

lightweight stick

Poke a hole through paper to attached flying string

Hold sticks together with ties or lightweight wire

Back of kite

Cut out pattern, then fold paper over string and tape.

String to create frame of kite

Fold tape over ends to hold string in place

Attach the tail of your kite here

Ingenious! Absolutely INGENIOUS!

Building on History!

Like most inventors, Orville and Wilbur were building ideas based on history. The brothers were certainly not the first to want to fly! During their studies, they learned a great deal about the history of man's attempt to achieve flight. Some of it was serious. Some was silly. People pursued flying even before there was written history to record their efforts.

Which Came First?

Look at the various types of aircraft below. In the small boxes, number the order in which these flying machines were invented!

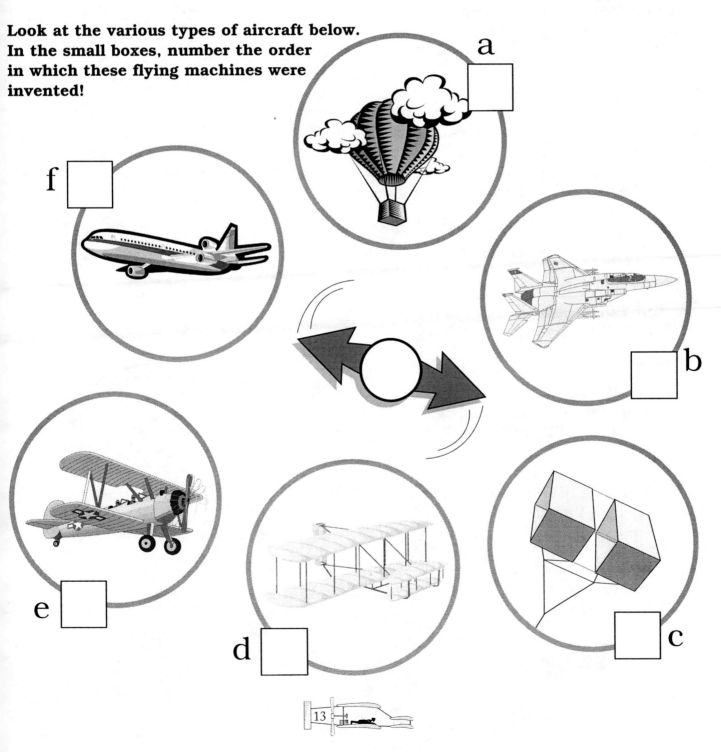

The Struggle With the Science!

As Orville and Wilbur Wright continued their work, they realized that they had to get the "science" of flight right to achieve their goals. From the very start, they tried to not only fly their backyard kites, but to control them while they were in the air. They believed that a glider could fly for a longer time if a pilot was controlling the airplane.

One day, Wilbur had one of those "Eureka!" moments! The brothers knew that when air moved over a wing that was "warped" (curved at the top), that it provided "lift" to the wing. And, *hmmm* . . . lift is what could help get a glider off the ground and keep it in the sky longer. Could, they wondered, a pilot control the "lift" of an aircraft?

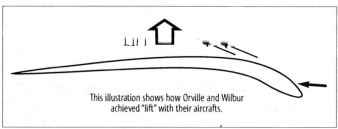

This illustration shows how Orville and Wilbur achieved "lift" with their aircrafts.

Wing Warping!

One of the most important things that Orville and Wilbur Wright figured out is that how the pressure of air acts over different shapes of wings is very important to a craft's ability to fly. They called this "wing warping." Also, it helps if you can control the wing! Look at the sketches below and answer the wing warping questions.

Circle one answer for each question:

Tug on the lines on the left side of the wing; this should turn your airplane:
LEFT   RIGHT   UP   DOWN

Pull the lines that control the right side of the wing; this will turn the plane:
RIGHT   LEFT   DOWN   UP

Pull on both lines at the same time to increase the "lift" of your plane.
This will cause the aircraft to go:
HIGHER   LOWER   SIDEWAYS   DOWNWARDS

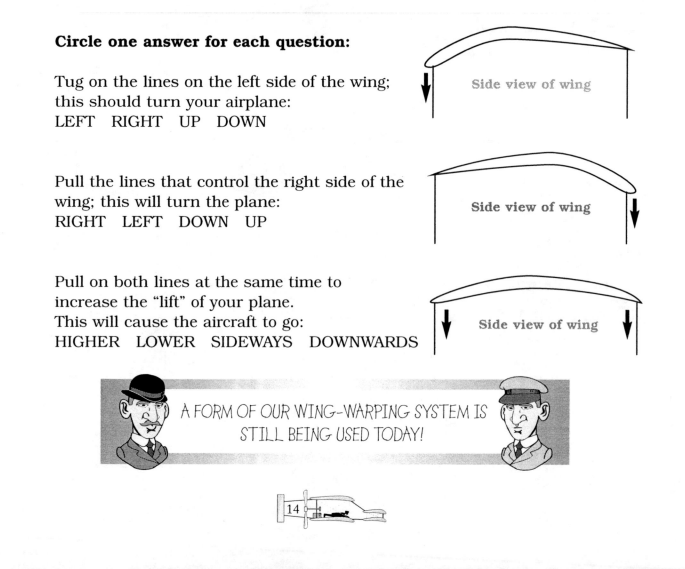

A FORM OF OUR WING-WARPING SYSTEM IS STILL BEING USED TODAY!

Warp Speed, Orville!

In their bicycle shop, the Wright brothers got busy. They built a glider that they believed would test the new principle of "wing warping." Then, they took the glider apart and packed it in pieces in a big, sturdy box.

A glider needs wind to get off the ground. Where, the brothers wondered, could they find a place where the wind blew almost all the time? Orville and Wilbur wrote the United States Weather Bureau in Washington, D.C. and asked them this very question. The answer? Kitty Hawk, North Carolina!

Because the tiny coastal town of Kitty Hawk was located beside the Atlantic Ocean, the sands there enjoyed an almost constant sea breeze. And sand? Why there were enormous sand dunes—one once grew so big that it finally blew right over a large hotel and gobbled it right up! One of these 100-feet-tall dunes was named Kill Devil Hill.

After Wilbur made a trip to check out the place, he and Orville packed up their glider, boarded a train, and headed for the coast of North Carolina . . . where history would soon be made!

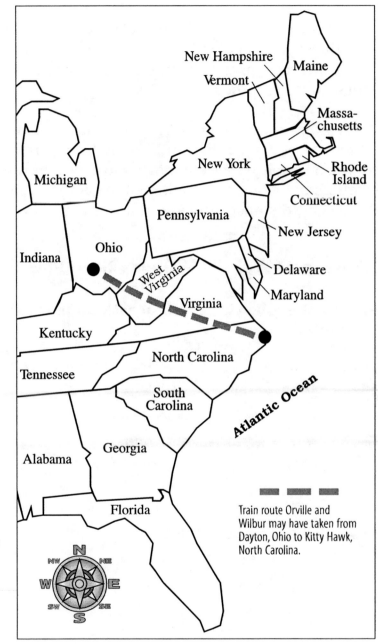

Train route Orville and Wilbur may have taken from Dayton, Ohio to Kitty Hawk, North Carolina.

Look at the sketch and answer the following questions:

1. Orville and Wilbur traveled through _____ _____ and _____ by train to get to Kitty Hawk.

2. North Carolina is by this body of water: _____ _____

3. Once they completed their flight, Orville and Wilbur returned home to _____.

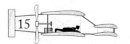

Those Amazing Young Men and Their Flying Machine!

At Kitty Hawk, Orville and Wilbur set up a tent to live in and began to experiment with their glider. Lo and behold, it worked! Just as they expected, one of them could lay face downward on the glider, catch the offshore breeze, tug at the lines to control the wings, and fly in the air over the sand!

However, their flights were very short, lasting only five to ten seconds and going only 20 to 30 feet across the sand. Nonetheless, their experiments that winter gave them confidence that they were moving in the right direction. As they practiced "flying," the brothers made a list of additional ideas that they thought would improve their aircraft and the height, distance, and speed it might achieve.

Orville and Wilbur—Mathematical Whizzes!

Answer the following math questions that the Wright brothers might have encountered.

1 If Orville flew 20 feet in 5 seconds, he was traveling _____ feet-per-second.

2 If Wilbur traveled 30 feet across the sand in 10 seconds, he was moving at _____ feet-per-second.

3 Orville's famous first flight went 120 feet. Wilbur's longer flight later that day was 852 feet. Wilbur traveled _____ feet farther than Orville.

4 Orville was in the air 12 seconds. Wilbur was in the air 59 seconds. Altogether they spent _____ seconds flying!

5 *Flyer* was about 40 feet long and cost $1,000 to build. That was about $____ ____ per foot.

6 *Flyer* weighed about 575 pounds. Orville weighed about 175 pounds. Altogether, the pilot had to get _____ pounds up into the air!

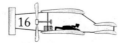

Oh, Won't Winter Ever Come?

The Wright brothers returned home to build a better glider. To help further understand the dynamics of flight, they built a wind tunnel. This was a box that was open at both ends. At one end, they placed a fan which created a steady stream of "wind" inside the box. Next, they wired model gliders inside the box to watch how they reacted to the wind. The information they gained through observing the different types of gliders helped them build a much better glider than the one they had used the winter before. In 1901, Orville and Wilbur returned to Kitty Hawk where they broke a world record for glider flight—389 feet!

Blowing in the Wind!

We built a model of the Wright Brothers Flyer to test in our wind tunnel. Look at the diagrams to answer the following questions.

1. Airplane number 1 is traveling in which direction?_____

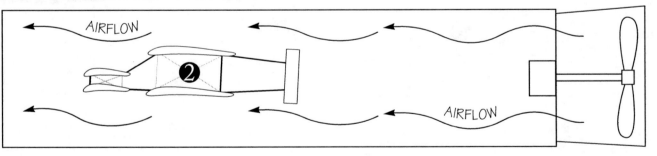

2. Airplane number 2 is traveling in which direction?_____

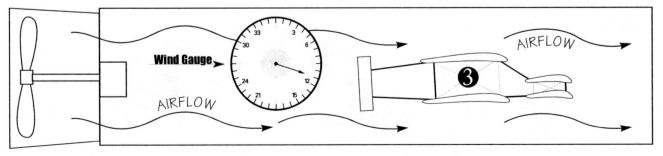

3. Airplane number 3 is traveling *with* the wind, but at twice the speed of the wind, so it is moving at _____ feet-per-minute.

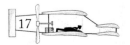

4. Airplane number 4 is traveling *against* the wind. It is twice as slow as airplane number 3. The plane is traveling at _____ feet-per-minute.

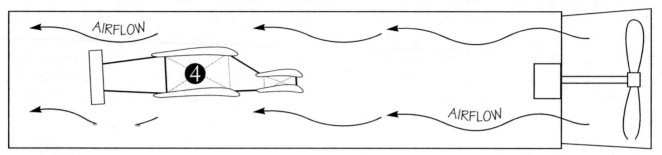

5. Airplane number 5 is traveling twice as fast as airplane number 3. Airplane 5 is traveling at _____ feet-per-minute.

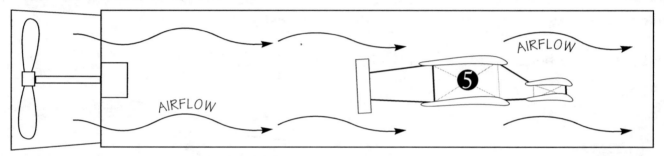

6. Airplane 6 is spiraling out of control! It is ____ ____ ____ ____ ____ ____ ____ that will bring it to earth—good thing it has no pilot!

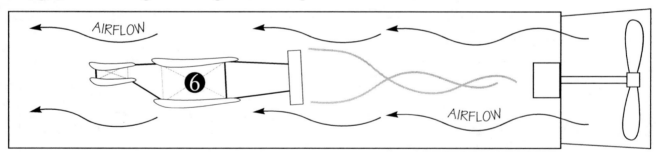

The Visitor

Once more, Orville and Wilbur went back to Dayton to improve on their efforts. They built a new glider that had a rudder. The rudder, along with the wing warping, would help control the glider even better. It didn't hurt that Orville was becoming more skilled as a pilot with each flight he made. Wilbur cheered him on in the winter of 1902. That winter, they glided an incredible 600 feet across Kill Devil Hill!

However, that was the problem—they were still "gliding," not truly flying. This was pointed out to them by a very special visitor to Kitty Hawk. Octave Chanute was a rich and famous engineer. He was twice as old as the Wright brothers, had a lot more education, had built and flown many gliders, and had even written a book that Orville and Wilbur had read. Imagine their surprise when this man showed up to admire, praise, and encourage these two young men!

Mr. Chanute told them something that the brothers already knew in their heads and hearts—they had achieved all they could with a glider. "Put a motor on your glider and turn it into a real airplane," the man advised them.

And Orville and Wilbur went home to their bike shop and did just that!

Circle the following attributes that play an important role in achieving success:

PATIENCE COMPLAINING
MISTAKES FAILURE LAZINESS
ENCOURAGEMENT
PERSEVERANCE GIVING UP
TIME EXCUSES WHINING
OPTIMISM BRAINSTORMING

Va-va-va-vrooooooooom!

From kite to glider to powered aircraft, that was Orville's and Wilbur's challenge! A kite is light. So is a glider. But when you added a heavy motor, this changed their equation of flight. What to do?

In a familiar pattern, the brothers wrote letters. However, no auto company was able to build an engine light enough to mount on an airplane. So, the brothers pulled out books and studied engines, then experimented with building one of their own.

First, they built a four-cylinder gasoline engine that weighed 150 pounds. Next, they built a propeller. This was not just any propeller! It was a propeller designed to their own specific specifications, greatly different from the "airscrews" other people had designed. Their propeller was designed much like the warped wings they had made, so that the propeller also created lift over its curved top and flat bottom. Today, airplane propellers are still pretty much designed along the principles that the Wright brothers developed in their bike shop!

Mechanical Matching!

Match the pictures with the word that most accurately describes them!

1. ____ straight wing

2. ____ bicycle

3. ____ propeller

4. ____ kite

5. ____ warped wing

6. ____ rudder

7. ____ glider

8. ____ engine

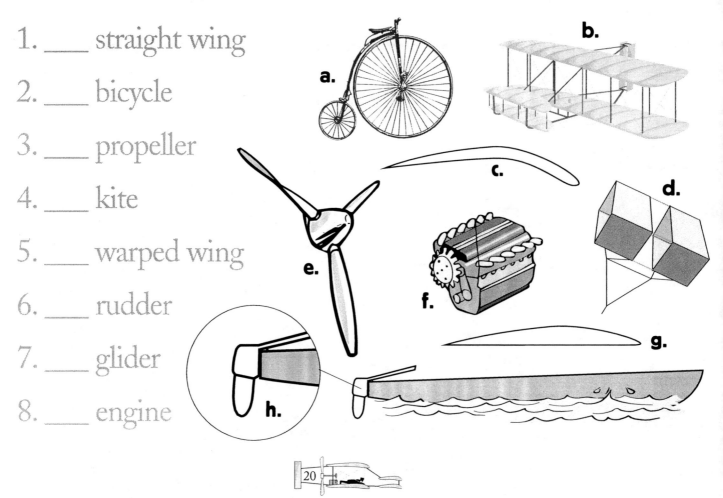

It Happened at Kitty Hawk!

On December 17, 1903, after a lifetime of dreams and thousands of trial flights including many failures—history was made!

It was made like a lot of history is made—with no one particularly paying attention! The day was so cold that puddles of water in the sand had frozen during the night. The chill wind, whisking along at 27-miles-an-hour, made it a miserable morning to make history.

Nonetheless, the brothers felt more than stinging cold sand in the air. They must have felt almost certain of success. We know this because they asked one of their helpers to make a photograph of the *Flyer* as soon as it lifted off.

This picture of the first flight was taken as Wilbur looks on from the ground.

Although the "first flight" was indeed a success, it would be years before most people around the world realized and understood the miracle that had taken place at Kitty Hawk that day. But Orville and Wilbur knew.

A Picture of Success!

Look at the photo above and answer the following questions, based on what you have read in this book.

1. _____ is flying the airplane.

2. The name of the airplane is ___ ___ ___ ___ ___.

3. This type of airplane is called a ___ ___ ___ ___ ___ ___.

4. The plane is flying on this sand dune: ___ ___ ___ ___

   ___ ___ ___ ___   ___ ___ ___ ___.

5. This historic event is happening in a place called

   ___ ___ ___ ___ ___   ___ ___ ___ ___.

6. The date is December 17, ___ ___ ___ ___.

7. The importance of this event is that it is the first time that man did this: ___ ___ ___.

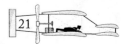

Fame and Fortune?—NOT!

What did Orville and Wilbur Wright do after their amazing success at Kitty Hawk that would change the course of world history? They went home. You might think that newspaper headlines would have read: FIRST FLIGHT BY WRIGHT! WORLD TO CHANGE FOREVER! But this was not so. Mostly, their amazing feat was ignored!

Fame and Fortune—Finally!

Help Orville and Wilbur tell their amazing success story of the first flight to the world by completing the front page of the newspaper below!

1. Masthead (Name of newspaper-make one up!)

2. Date Happened (Write on this line.)

3. Dateline (Place where happened)

4. BIG HEADLINE!

5. Tell the news!

6. Photo (Draw the picture from page 23 in upper right box.)

7. Sidebar (Put a quotation or trivia fact in lower right box.)

8. Editor (Hey, that's you!)

I can't wait to read your story!

Did you know!...

Editor:

THE WRIGHT COMPANY

In 1909, Orville and Wilbur formed the Wright Company. They opened a factory in Dayton where they would produce airplanes. The U. S. Army expressed interest in buying Wright airplanes. Indeed, the brothers received orders for airplanes from all around the world! For so many years, the brothers had invested their own time, effort, and money in the hopes of advancing flight to something others could see, understand, and use. Now, it appeared, they would get a return on their investment.

The Right Company at the Right Time!

Match the aircraft with their correct name.

____ 1. The "Around the World in 80 Days" Hot Air Balloon

____ 2. The French/British *Concorde*

____ 3. The Spirit of St. Louis

____ 4. Blackhawk Helicopter

____ 5. The Hindenburg Dirigible

____ 6. Harrier Jet

____ 7. Stealth Bomber

b.

a.

d.

c.

g.

e.

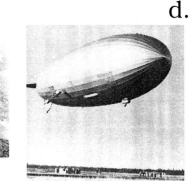

f.

Here, There, Everywhere—Airplanes!

It was pretty incredible how quickly flight advanced after the Wright brothers' success at Kitty Hawk. By the time Orville Wright died in 1948, he had lived long enough to see:

- Larger airplanes with enclosed cockpits and cabins for passengers
- Even larger airplanes with as many as four engines that could carry even more people, farther distances, at faster speeds
- The advent of jet engines and the breaking of the sound barrier

Of course, this was not the end of the story! Rocket engines! Aircraft traveling at supersonic speeds! Jet engine helicopters! Stealth fighter jets! Harrier jets that can take off straight up! Shuttles to space! And an airplane—the *Concorde*—that can fly at twice the speed of sound, traveling from New York to London or Paris in just a little over three short hours!

Why, what would Orville and Wilbur think about all of this? Would they be surprised? I doubt it!

Flight in the Future!

Draw your version of an aircraft we might see in the year 2050!

Memorials and More!

In 1953, 29 years after their famous first flight, an enormous granite memorial built atop Kill Devil Hill was dedicated to Orville and Wilbur Wright. Another memorial to the Wright brothers is located in the National Air and Space Museum in Washington, D.C. This museum, part of the Smithsonian Institution, is where the original *Flyer* hangs as a reminder of the history that took place one cold winter's day at Kitty Hawk.

DOT-DOT-DOT, DASH-DASH!

Connect the dots and dashes to discover the objects below, then write their names on the lines provided!

__ __ __ __ __ __ __ __ __

__ __ __ __ __ __ __ __ __

Memorial

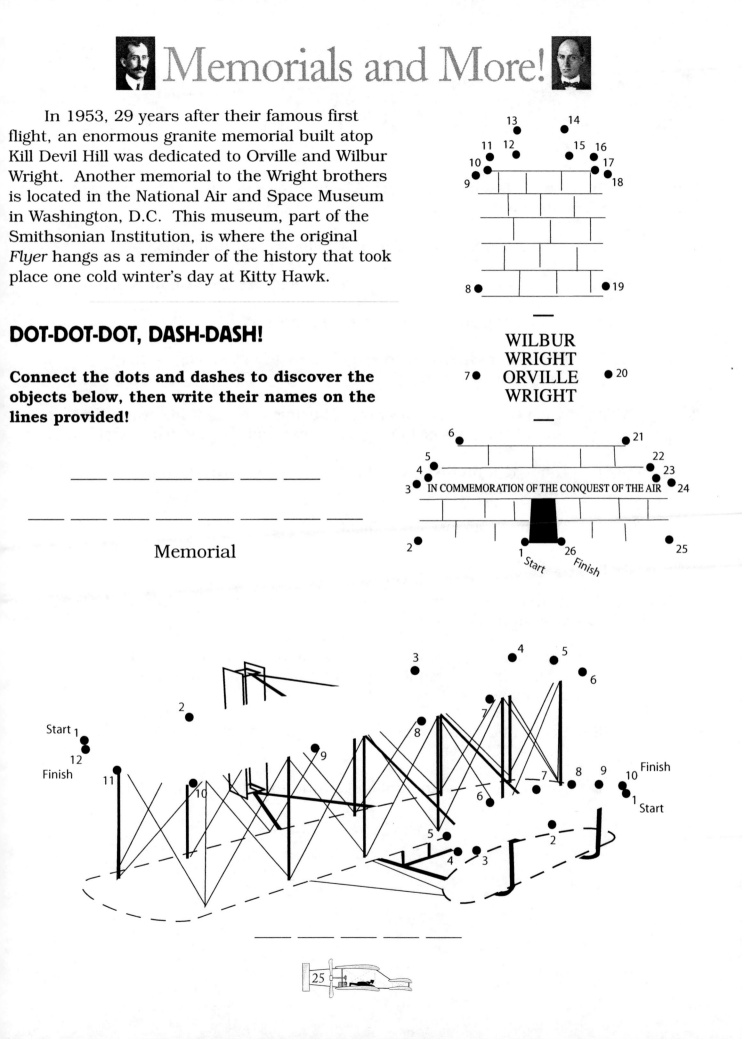

WILBUR
WRIGHT
ORVILLE
WRIGHT

IN COMMEMORATION OF THE CONQUEST OF THE AIR

Start   Finish

__ __ __ __ __ __

Wright Brothers and First Flight Trivia!

Orville and Wilbur were fascinating guys! Circle T for True or F for False, whichever you believe about the trivia below!

TRUE / FALSE   Wilbur was born in Indiana; Orville was born in Ohio.

TRUE / FALSE   Their father was a bishop of the United Brethren Church.

TRUE / FALSE   Neither boy graduated from high school!

TRUE / FALSE   As children, they earned spending money by selling mechanical toys they made at home.

TRUE / FALSE   When Orville started a printing business, he built his own printing press out of items that included a beat-up trombone and parts of old buggies.

TRUE / FALSE   The Wright brothers tested more than 200 different wing models in their wind tunnel.

TRUE / FALSE   They made almost 1,000 flights in their 1902 glider.

TRUE / FALSE   *Flyer* cost less than $1,000 to build.

TRUE / FALSE   In 1908, Orville crashed a plane in Virginia; he was hurt and a passenger was killed.

TRUE / FALSE   *Flyer* was made of wooden poles, baling wire, muslin cloth, bicycle chains, and a gasoline engine that had no more power than a lawn mower!

TRUE / FALSE   Orville and Wilbur flipped a coin to see who got to make the historic flight at Kitty Hawk.

TRUE / FALSE   Wilbur once flew an airplane around the Statue of Liberty!

How many did you get right?

Two Days That Were Different in the History of Flight

Orville and Wilbur Wright's successful first flight on December 17, 1903 was a joyful event. They both believed that one day airplanes would be used to transport passengers and mail. However, I'm sure they never imagined a day like September 11, 2001 when airplanes were used by terrorists as weapons of war. Write a letter to Orville and Wilbur telling them of the good and bad things that airplanes have meant to mankind.

AIR MAIL

Dear Sirs,

_____

_____

_____

_____

_____

_____

_____

_____

Sincerely yours,

Four men and one boy witnessed the famous flight that took place at Kitty Hawk on December 17, 1903. Perhaps this is how he might have recalled the milestone morning.

Write your own poem about the famous flight on the tablet below.

Child of Flight

Mr. Orville, Mr. Wilbur, all of us up early;
Me and the grown up men
Left the lifesaving station—
Would there be a life to save on the sand?

What is this flying all about, I wonder;
Birds and kites, I can see, but men?
Mr. Orville, Mr. Wilbur, they believe

Ice on the ground, frost in the air;
Mr. Orville, Mr. Wilbur, they shake hands;
The machine they call *Flyer* sits on the sand;
Now a man climbs aboard;
Machine and man seem one

The noise of the engine, the noise of the wind;
We tug the *Flyer* along its track until, until,
Until . . .It lets loose upon the sky!

Mr. Orville, Mr. Wilbur, what have they done?
Dad says made history, all will change.
Me and the grown up men
Trudge through the sand

Back to the lifesaving station,
I note in the log:
Mr. Orville, Mr. Wilbur fly at Kitty Hawk;
No lives lost today

I wish I had been there!

Me, too!

Celebrate!: The 100th Anniversary of the Birth of Flight

 From December 17, 2002 to December 17, 2003, you will see many celebrations of Orville and Wilbur Wright's famous first flight at Kitty Hawk. Here are some ways you might find to celebrate FLIGHT!

 Visit The Wright Brothers National Memorial in Kitty Hawk, North Carolina.

 Visit these places in Dayton, Ohio: Aviation Trail; Carillon Historical Park; Dayton Aviation Heritage National Historical Park; Montgomery County Historical Society's Old Courthouse Museum; U.S. Air Force Museum; Dayton-Wright Brothers Airport.

 In Dearborn, Michigan at the Henry Ford Museum and Greenfield Village, see the original Wright Cycle Shop and their boyhood home, moved here from Dayton.

 In Washington, D.C., go to the National Air and Space Museum to see the original 1903 *Flyer!*

 Collect newspaper and magazine clippings about how others are celebrating the birth of flight. For example, two Cornelia, Georgia brothers (named Wright!) plan to take off and land their airplane at every U.S. public airport with a paved runway!

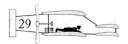

Additional Resources to Explore!

BOOKS

Before the Wright Brothers by Don Berliner

Wilbur, Orville and the Flying Machine by Max Marquardt

The Wright Brothers by Anna Sproule

The Wright Brothers and Aviation by Steve Parker

The Wright Brothers at Kitty Hawk by Donald Sobol

Young Orville and Wilbur Wright: First to Fly by Andrew Woods

LIBRARIES

Special Collections and Archives

Paul Laurence Dunbar Library

Wright State University

Dayton, Ohio

Kitty Hawk Public Library

Kitty Hawk, North Carolina

WEBSITES

www.hfmgv.org

www.nasm.si.edu

www.wpafb.af.mil/museum

www.firstflightcentennial.org

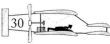

Glossary

attributes: (ah treh BUTES) characteristics; things that make up a person's character

entrepreneur: (an truh pra nure) a person who takes an idea and turns it into a business, usually in spite of many setbacks and obstacles

eureka: (you REE kah) a Greek word meaning, "I found it!"

failure: evidence that something does not work in a particular way at one particular time (meaning it might work some other way or this way some other time, so keep trying!)

glider: an aircraft that has no motor but flies only by the force of the wind

mechanical: (muh CAN eh kul) something made or that operates using mechanics; can be a simple toy, or as complex as a jet airplane

mode: (MOWED) a way or a method of doing something

ornithopter: (or nuh THOP tur) an early version of the helicopter

rudder: used in boats and airplanes to help control the direction of the craft

success: achievement of a goal in spite of obstacles and setbacks; often takes many years and is not immediately appreciated by others

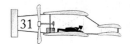

Answer Key

page 10: 1-c; 2-b; 3-a
page 11: 1-e; 2-d; 3-c; 4-f; 5-a; 6-b
page 13: c, a, d, e, f, b
page 14: LEFT, RIGHT, HIGHER
page 15: West Virginia, Virginia;
        Atlantic Ocean; Ohio
page 16: 1-4; 2-3; 3-732; 4-71; 5-$25.00; 6-750
page 17/18: 1-east; 2-west; 3-22; 4-5.5;
            5-44; 6-gravity

page 19: patience, mistakes, failure,
encouragement, perseverance, time, optimism,
brainstorming
page 20: 1-g; 2-a; 3-e; 4-d; 5-c; 6-h; 7-b; 8-f
page 21: 1-Orville; 2-Flyer; 3-glider; 4-Kill Devil;
        5-Kitty Hawk; 6-1903; 7-fly
page 23: 1-f; 2-a; 3-e; 4-b; 5-d; 6-g; 7-c
page 25: Wright Brothers, Flyer
page 26: All are true!

Index

Photo Credit:
Page 9, Dayton Metro Library